Lowcountry

OTHER BOOKS BY
JOHN ALLMAN

POETRY

Walking Four Ways in the Wind
Clio's Children: Dostoevsky at Semyonov Square
and Other Poems
Scenarios for a Mixed Landscape
Curve Away from Stillness: Science Poems
Inhabited World: New & Selected Poems 1970-1995
Loew's Triboro
Attractions
(a chapbook of prose poems)

FICTION

Descending Fire & Other Stories

Lowcountry

POEMS BY

JOHN ALLMAN

A NEW DIRECTIONS BOOK

Book design by Sylvia Frezzolini Severance
Manufactured in the United Sates of America
New Directions Books are printed on acid-free paper.
Published simultaneously in Canada by Penguin Books Canada Limited.

Grateful acknowledgment is made to W. W. Norton & Co. for permission to quote
The Journal of Charlotte L. Forten, ed. Ray Allen Billington,
1981, copyright 1953 by the Dryden Press, Inc.

Library of Congress Cataloging-in-Publication Data

Allman, John, 1935–
    Lowcountry : poems / by John Allman.
        p. cm.
    ISBN 978-0-8112-1710-1 (pbk. : acid-free paper)
    1. South Carolina—Poetry. I. Title.

PS3551.L46L69 2007
811'.54—dc22
                                           2007026880

New Directions Books are published for James Laughlin
by New Directions Publishing Corporation,
80 Eighth Avenue, New York, NY 10011

This book is for my granddaughters,

Katherine and Viktoria

TABLE OF CONTENTS

LEAVING HOME

1999

This Time   2

Chameleon   3

Biking the Course   4

Renters   5

Journal   6

Dust   7

The Art League Gallery   8

Reading Andrew Marvell   9

All Night the Wind   10

Dream   11

Chameleons   12

Heron on the Bridge   13

LEAVING HOME

2000

Guests   16

Swash Line   17

Syntax   19

Conversation   21

Dream   23

Reading Paul Gauguin   24

The Beach at Windsor Place   25

The Music of Osun   26

Moon   28

Crossing the Folly   30

LEAVING HOME

2001

Dream   35

Outsider Art   36

Watching the Medieval Mystery Plays
   and Thinking of Milton   37

News from Home   38

Reflections   39

Trio   40

"You Ain't Hurryin' Me"   43

Reading Czeslaw Milosz   44

LEAVING HOME

2002

Singleton Beach   46

Boundaries   47

Dream   48

In the Gullah Flea Market   49

Outlet Mall   51

Reading Tennessee Williams   52

Preserve   53

Scenes from the Passing World   54

LEAVING HOME
2003

A Broken Stair   58

The Sighting   59

De Blue Keeps D'Em Haints Away   60

Construction   61

Entries   63

Dream   65

Reading Marianne Moore   66

Rapture   67

News from Home   68

LEAVING HOME
2004

Reading Jorie Graham   70

Watching Weather   71

In the Forest   72

Dream   73

Twins   74

Crime Report   75

Neuropathy   76

Feast   77

Key West   78

For the Umpteenth Time   80

Dancing Gull   82

Return   83

ACKNOWLEDGMENTS

Grateful acknowledgment is made to those journals who first published some of these poems: *5 AM,* "Outsider Art"; *Beloit Poetry Journal,* "Syntax"; *Blackbird: an online journal of literature and the arts,* "News from Home," "Reading Andrew Marvell," "Renters," "This Time"; *Ekphrasis, "Feast"*; *Futurecycle,* "Journal," "Key West," "Rapture"; *Kestrel,* "Scenes from the Passing World"; *The Taj Mahal Review,* "A Broken Stair," "Singleton Beach."

37 of the poems appeared as an electronic chapbook, *Lowcountry,* published by the online journal *Mudlark* as its issue #31, edited by William Slaughter.

The quotes in "Journal" from Charlotte L. Fortren are taken from *The Journals of Charlotte L. Fortren,* ed. Ray Allen Billington. W.W. Norton & Company, 1981.

In "Conversation," "The slave children..." paragraph is from the account of Mary Anderson, and the "Harriet Beecher Stowe..." paragraph is from the account of Thomas Hall, both accounts occurring in *My Folks Don't Want Me to Talk About Slavery: Twenty-one Oral Histories of Former North Carolina Slaves,* ed. Belinda Hurmence. John F. Blair, publisher, 1984.

For some of the biological detail in these poems I am indebted to the wonderful book by Todd Ballantine, *Tideland Treasure,* revised edition. University of South Carolina Press, 1991.

I am grateful to Barbara and Peter Tobias for allowing us to spend winters in their home at 1 St. George Road, where many of these poems were brought to completion.

Peter Glassgold, Peter Johnson and Jay Meek have read these poems at various stages and given me their wisdom and advice, for which I am more than appreciative. Dan Masterson scoured the manuscript word by word, and I toiled until Eileen gave the book her blessing.

Lowcountry

LEAVING HOME

1999

This is the drive into the story, the wet
road unfurling in our rearview mirror,
where we say good-bye to friends whose
walkers snag on carpets, good-bye to the
vet's needle anaesthetizing our cats, their
bleeding gums; our own x-rays put off
another year; family fetes, the fear of our
not returning, also postponed another year—
the narrative now urgent to get back to its
beginning, afraid of being discovered, always
going the other way, hoping to be abandoned.
We see it only in our leaving—the white wing
that sweeps across the sky, carrying before it
the breath of departure, an inflated syntax,
the emptiness of clouds . . .

THIS TIME

Think if the first garden began along the sea:
ducks, cormorants, loons, terns navigating
from the north to be named in this place for
long neck or *frightening cry*, the *quick dive*,
the sudden *attitude in wind*, our slow progress
over the bridge from the mainland the untying
of the tongue. Adam never saw a bull thistle
in his life—or sea rocket or stinkhorn or beach
pennywort—the heron stabbing snakes, while Eve,
glistening with sweat, dreamt the long waters

of Calibogue Sound, even when Skull Creek
was veering east before any bridge threw its
shadow down. The tide bringing us this far
salty as blood. A froth. A whiteness. Pale eyes.
We're pointing at the great blue heron gliding
full-length over the marsh, trailing its history
of crawling things that disdained the ground,
its shadow slicing the lagoon that separates
condo from house from shack, our sentences
falling apart. "Look! Look!" The heron gone.

CHAMELEON

Beau, our black cat, holds it gingerly
in his mouth, its legs protruding. I try
to extract it by the tail, but the tail
snicks off, falls wriggling to the carpet,
tossing and turning, while the body it
came from goes comatose in Beau's
bewildered mouth. He drops it. Pokes
the tail. Backs off puzzled by this
cold-blooded shivering of something
so disembodied. So small. So wormlike.
A thin mad finger flexing and pointing.
A green thread plucked from a god's garment,
alive because anything that touches divinity
lives. Its partial truth the mystery of motion
without heart or brain, the body it came from
used to altering itself on rotted wood or stone
or twig, turning brown or puce, its altered colors
on myrtle leaf the afterthought of common
belonging. And when Beau and I look up,
the chameleon is gone, splayed wet footprints
leading to the deck, the myrtle poking
between slats, and who knows what slither
causing light to slide down the western sky.

BIKING THE COURSE

We're here without permission, without documents,
not allowed this grunt and shove around golf
cart paths that snake in and out of live oak, pine,
magnolia. Doves flutter above our spattery approach,
but we're not the only people in drizzle and gray.
A man in yellow slicker teeing off by himself,
ball after ball flying into the mist, into next week's
flow chart, the plunk of deficits. Someone's Irish
setter prances around us as we peddle toward
the far edge: St. Andrews' villas, one under another,
lights hung from rented ceilings, our caps dripping,
where this morning two women emerged from their
cart carefully plotting the lay of putts, the kiss
of club, each of their balls quietly entering the tiny
dark hole of happiness. A great blue heron stands
at pond's edge, watching herself descend into the
wavering village on the surface, lit windows there,
her twin rising to meet her, long legs telescoping
into each other, dimpling water now the shatter
of rain, as we peddle faster, afraid of not breaking
through, not coming out of that drowned city
beneath the reflection of our pumping legs, breath
steaming, trying to get back to where we belong.

RENTERS

The egret's platform of sticks no more permanent
than my furnished room on West 58th Street—
that shared toilet a marsh creek or slough
rich in mice. Think how all the wading birds
like to breed near each other, regurgitating night
and day into the maws of their young. Think of
the apartments we inhabited on busy avenues,
the honking of cars trapped by double parkers,
the attic rooms with low dormers we hit our heads on,
the ghastly abstract mural a tenant painted on the green wall,
its pretension of vitality and swirl and soft mire
where the bittern coughs. Think how the ring-billed
gull returns north, replenishing itself on farmers' pests,
how we abandoned the Bronx to arrive on a snow-filled
midnight in Syracuse, our goods on the sidewalk like twigs
for the picking.

JOURNAL

*"Have passed Edisto and several other islands and can now see
Hilton Head. . . . The South Carolina shore is flat and low;—a long
line of trees. It does not look very inviting."*

Charlotte L. Forten,
Oct. 28, 1862

What's war, when the land blooms? *This afternoon
went into the woods, and gathered some casino berries
and beautiful magnolia leaves and exquisite ferns.
How beautifully they contrast, on my table, with the daffodils
and narcissus.* In the marsh, a shred of a girl's dress,
her sister's stocking, where they sank and yet swam
into a father's arms. The sight of black troops: certain
white women *vented their spleen . . . telling them they ought
to be at work in their masters' rice swamps, and that they
ought to be lashed to death.* Stain, scar, lash-infested
wound not nearly a vocabulary for the *strange wild dream
from which I am constantly expecting to escape.*

This evening, over a hundred years later, I try to sleep.
A serrated tumble of pine cones on the roof, a child's
thin voice rising in the distance, where perfection fails.

DUST

We're renting on the edge of the 14th tee; a large pond
where ibises poke for bugs and snails, the faint *thwack*
of club meeting ball like small-arms fire in the distance.
The real urgency not carts humming from sand hazard
to hole. It's the breeze blowing dust through window
screens, the yellow pollen of oak, sycamore, sweet
birch and pine coating the glass coffee table, our
books, the rounded ceramic lamps, these particles,
this miniscule soot that is the saffron powder on the
red hood of our Taurus, the fragile pink surface of your
breathing. There is no remedy for stories of suffocation,
air washed by acid rain, the flight of a ball outside
like something expelled from its original intent—
white nippled hardness, severed knuckle, the soft fall
onto perfect grass, where darkness crouches, asthmatic
and insolvent among blade after blade giving off seed,
slash, bruise, the inflamed gism and surrender that carry
the tardy genius of oxygen into your needful blood.
Breathe. Breathe. Breathe. Breathe. Breathe. Breathe.

Someone has framed the primal detritus of life slipping just
below the surface, bubbling in decay. No humans gawking
except at these canvases, their wine purpling in plastic glasses,
bits of cheese falling like deciduous sayings, an "Ahh," an "Ooh"
gentle as the breeze leaning salt grass to the tide. Sunsets. More
marshes. Their creators a retired dentist. A silver-haired CEO.
A widow with two labradors. A music teacher's clumps of
spartina, egrets settling behind them, fair and soft spoken
as greeting cards in Walgreen's. They're beginners who've lived
long enough to want the world tactile beyond harm. To show
faint yellows in a Provençal landscape, a mill pond reflecting
the unshuttered windows of their youth. Take this "Moment in
Time," by a former magistrate, the years of her South Dakota
winters blown out between the palmettos on either side of a lagoon,
the sea hinted at in the distance grown cerise with sinking vagaries
of the sun, like the appeals of those who appeared before her,
facts as calm as the still life of pears. The bland faults of ridged
impasto and jarring colors the not yet broken habits of a lifetime's labor.

READING ANDREW MARVELL

Forget parallel lines that never meet
when every surface is flat. Recall the
summer our daughter learned to swim
at Lake Dutchess, dogpaddling to the float.
I cut the first lawn while tottering on the
riding mower, going round and round.
Paradise like that. Repetitive. Look at
the perfectly tapered wren fly up into the live

oak tangled in Spanish moss and listen to its
small song. It rains and we go inside, towel
off, we make love, something sputtering to life,
that noise like a wheel wobbling on the mower
I steered up and down the yard I had just
scythed clear of wild carrot, wild mustard.
Here the souls of things struggle into their sheaths,
grow tinsel wings, flutter upward to sit and stare,

the lagoon's shimmer in apposition to the stars.

ALL NIGHT THE WIND

All night the wind, the frantic crepe myrtle snapping
off its thinnest branches. The world again so round
what I felt last week is here again, my father risen
from paralysis, his gaunt face smiling. Think of this
clam worm projecting its tube out of the sand, its many-
haired length, the meat it crunches in its horny jaws,
how at night it leaves its cylindrical burrow to feed
in the sea, the special sensors on its head fondling prey,
how in summer it will mate and die, washed ashore,
its pitiful anger at the sun not at all what I have in mind
this morning, the curve of the earth gleaming in the dividing
light where water ends.

DREAM

Feeling the warmth of their arms around me, I'm embracing old friends missing for years, the college boy I was, selling watered-down drinks in Carnegie Hall, Bartok's music a passion of claws scratching down a wall, all of us dressed as lawyers, shrinks, poets, talking a storm. I'm 22 and tan, in California again, my co-worker at Shamban Engineering with a '57 Plymouth's fins like something from outer space, bright sun sizzling our eyes, we argue Sputnik and girls. A sonic boom overhead as a fighter peels off over the Pacific. I'm caught standing in the Freeway, a red MG sports car brushing past, its top down, an old man waving.

CHAMELEONS

These nights we awaken tinged from a place
staining words, the camellias nodding their
scarlet heads outside the window, azaleas
straining their stick souls to the limit of darkness,
faint purple seen beyond closed eyelids, past habits
of attachment, as if we clung to color to change
what we were. The word for ice spelling out
our years in Syracuse, when gray shards hung
from a church gable, our daughter just beginning
to talk, flattening her *a*'s in the back of our
old Chevy, crying that winter when timber
wolves sniffed her through the wire fence at the zoo.
Seen within that sky, we were bone against bone,
already reaching our hands toward a seeded future,
beyond the 14th tee, something flowering in our grasp,
a ghostly botany our bodies now emulate, so that
years and the distance traveled behind us become
a Doppler pursuit, whatever we might have been
or now will be closing upon us in blue robes of
acceptance. Think how many years ago I was the
gray of sickly elms on a busy Queens avenue,
before I dreamed of your wet thighs sparkling
on the float in the middle of Lake Peekskill,
a hope like porcelain held to the mirroring sky.
Just as this morning, the slow flap of ibises allows
them to halt almost mid-air, above the pond,
the live oaks less gnarled, more horizontal
to a need, never achieving it, against the dawn
that we are part of in this rising and rising.

HERON ON THE BRIDGE

Ancient as a pharaoh in robes, he stares
from the handrail meant to keep pedestrians
where they belong, something about humans
that perpetrates a fall. His attention a quiet,
steady flow above the sky-streaming lagoon.
Hunched shoulders. Stray feathers dangling
beneath the indifferent hardness of his
gaze. A kind of beard, unkempt wisdom,
brittle bony body an epitome of soul.
How do I greet him where I need to cross?

2000

What air! We're traveling between the twin harps
of the Memorial Bridge, descending
from another State, in the shrill rising
wail of our cats as we change altitudes—
traversing backwards the slave route and traps
of Maryland, Havre de Grace, the moods
Douglass carpentered into orotund
preaching, all those words he pried from the stunned
silence of the dead, words for being free;
in these times, fragile syllables that one
throws against the deaf walls of job and debt,
a small song to ward off calamity
of spirit. Later, crossing the Potomac:
Washington Monument; a bruised history
nothing like the sun in our eyes or my
struggle with the plastic-wrapped mobile home
swaying its wide load, hogging the tarmac,
family on the move, America grown
steep in hope, its visible soul finicky
as shifting wind, the lean hands steady
of a father steering east, west, while we quicken
south, brush past, wave to the couple smoking
in the cab of the truck hauling three-roomed
happiness, their solvency in motion.

GUESTS

The owner's family photos smiling in the living room,
happy landlords. These windows closed, I can't hear
the ocean, I don't remember any of our street names,
the forgetful beach three stories below giving more
and more of itself to receding tide so shallow I could
walk to the horizon and hardly cover my knees. I can
see you and Ruth Ann walking back from the Hyatt,
redwood chairs, redwood deck, workmen smearing
pungent sealer that takes her breath away. She stumbles
in the sand and you hold her around the waist like a
mother. No one knows why she's losing her voice,
why she faints in the bathroom, why she lived so many
years with a husband now behind me watching C-Span,
the senators trying to impeach someone for love that was
or is not love. Nor sex. Ruth Ann doesn't cry anymore.
Just emits a low wailing sound like something that
might be out there calling its mate, half out of water,
flailing the darkness below. I watch you take her
under an arm and navigate the sand giving way,
light pouring from the north, over Port Royal Sound,
bathing the afternoon in silence and recrimination.

SWASH LINE

It's not just where miles of dried
spartina stalks have been washed
into the tide and returned, making
rattan mats the gulls step on like
barefoot house boys, or the sinking
into the sand of tangled creatures
who couldn't let go,

or the way they heap as if piled
there by a copper-skinned man
gathering his roofing in a time
now as ceased as the midden shell
rings and the rose-colored sail
of his boat.

It's not the way a storm tide
thrashes white foam up and over
the lip formed by last year's dredge
spew, a renourished beach, these
desiccated reeds criss-crossed
and flattened into a seamstress's
edging suddenly spongy with salt vomit
and rain,

or the humiliating contrast
of the hotel's pots of hyacinths
blushing in the midst of dusty miller,
and the bordered mauve kale opening
like a girl's crinoline under the
palmettos.

The land drawing its line against a
sculpting ocean that eats into cliff,
that powders schist, hurling the
knobbed whelk out of dream,
castigating siphon-feeders and the
filtering soft-coin lives that attach
themselves to slippery stone, creating
a polis with a single, repetitive thought,

the moon crab slowly aslant
in its preoccupations, scrape-
sliding over husks once green
and high, swiveling stalked eyes
toward the surf, swinging about
on vibrations in the reeds,
the ground of its being held to
the land by the land's leavings,
as the sea whines like a dog.

SYNTAX

Reeds, mud grip, shell that forms only
upon shell, this marsh rising and falling
to sea-pulse, moon-drag: news of itself
the only front-page effort worth its
time. I'm bored with self, the drop-out
ego abashed at how little it confounds
the tide's insistence. I'm fed up with
a name lifting itself into the breeze
of opinion, the sky's azure only air
that curves to authoring roundness.
Nothing steps out of nature. Nothing
returns from the vast water that does
not crave its tidal beginning. Look
across Calibogue Sound, at the three-masted
dredge adding ocean floor to Daufuskie Island:
spewing sand and broken bi-valves, crackled
carapaces, torn whip coral, stag-horn
weed, the sea's waste like the mind's
creaturely ideas sinking to the bottom,
pulverized into voiceless god-ground poverty.
A turning over. Shuck and thrust. Hurled
column and collapse. A foothold reappearing
further from tidy lawns and a porch
filled with tourists in peaked caps, their
glinting binoculars tilted to a sight-line
low as this row of belly-wet pelicans
close to white-caps, profile pterodactyl,
their glide precise as a hand moving over

text, without hesitation, instincted
to its course. Sucking sound. Fume-moan.
Stinking blackness. Shuddering belts,
sudden fling: the given-up now the only
given.

"If *someone* or *something* didn't make," he said, "so many birds nearly alike, we wouldn't be saying, 'No, that one doesn't have the white throat or the black bill or the wind-blown tuft the back of its head,' just to explain exactness and the way we get to name quill and pimple and horny toe."

"Is that little dog deceased yet?"

"You know," she said, "I just love that skittery song the willets make when they open up their black-tipped wings and the sand-pipers go bunched over the water like a cloud of mosquitoes."

"The slave children all carried mussel shells in their hands to eat with. The food was put on large trays and the children all gathered around and ate, dipping up their food with their mussel shells, which they used as spoons."

"Listen," he said, "they might be widening the road to Beaufort, but I got three dollars says I get there just as fast by the power of my eternal mind."

"Harriet Beecher Stowe, the writer of *Uncle Tom's Cabin*, did that for her own good. She had her own interests at heart, and I don't like her. Lincoln, or none of the crowd. The Yankees helped free us, so they say, but they let us be put back in slavery again."

"Just listen to those people complaining," she said, "and I'll show you how embarrassed they should be, all red like that because they can't see the difference between ordinary shame and the natural beauty of fallen leaves turning ruby."

"If you don't have anything good to say about anybody, come sit by me."

DREAM

Biking on shell-crunch beach steering around tidal pools, salt on the chain, grit between my teeth. Men on scaffolds are spraying noxious sealant, stucco walls losing the color of their ivory skin, fumes like a thin logic that dries on the tongue. I saw my father injured in a truck accident, his ten-wheeler on its side, wheels spinning, sand leaking from the hopper that empties into a revolving drum, mixing with water and cement, his days hardened into the path I stepped off long ago. The blood down the side of his face raspberry and sweet, I ride effortlessly, north wind at my back. A burning something rising into the sinuses, around my eyes, blurring vision like eyeglasses greased by fingerprints. He looks away. He slips out of himself. He's gone. The spilled sand and blood spattering my legs as I pedal across a narrow channel.

READING PAUL GAUGUIN

He named his notebook *Noa Noa*, "fragrant
fragrant," a text for paradise, where pebbly ground
hardens one's feet, even as I shake sand out of my shoe.
    "Confusion of trees," bouraos, ironwood,
    pandanus, hibiscus, guava, giant leaves a canopy
    for bronze-limbed women adjusting red

blossoms behind their ears, all that joy
in roaming the forest, hatcheting a path.
His words follow me into afternoon, rocking
    from the sea, crumbling open on the beach,
    drifting down from scarred palmettos. Gauguin
    stepping out of his doorway naked

(the hole in this whelk the way it meets the world),

a wild silence descending on breadfruit
and fern, his 13-year-old wife smoking in bed,
her awareness beyond comprehension.
    The sea I walk along now less familiar,
    sleeplessness folding unseen into seen,
    the day's harmonies flattening into brown and blue,

the willet dipping toward its reflection in a tidal pool.

THE BEACH AT WINDSOR PLACE

Out of our shoes, across the dunes, watching
the curve of day sink its wheel rim rolling
into the sea, a crescent moon suddenly
crossed by four pelicans, swaying travelers
nearly asleep, though on the wing, their lives
threaded to a single beat. Something in the brain
disbelieves distance, a motion in the sky forever
near. Stillness destroyed in the surge at our feet,
as we step over carapace and weed through the portals
of blandness, striking down mild comparisons,
penetrating the sleep of gulls, something of us
tossed into the surge and returned, footprints swirling
in the signatures of bodies where we walk the wind,
the tide rocking forward, nothing but erasure on its mind.

THE MUSIC OF OSUN

After the painting by Arianne King Comer

Arianne's in the parking lot on the edge
of the Gullah Festival, helping white-haired
ladies imprint their own patterns for scarves—
her blue the color of their childhood lips
when they emerged from a Michigan lake
or walked along Kennesaw River
or the wind blew through their years
along the North Way.
                    Arianne's long braids
dangle free, almost sweeping the wet indigo
pads. A gospel group on the Festival platform
sings, "We're walkin' in the light,/ Let the light
shine over the world,/ We're walkin' in the light."

Inside "De Aarts Ob We People" exhibit,
I poke my head under Arianne's "Indigo
Tree," her splay of blues and greens, these colors
the hues of a people's clasp in that other land.
Makeshift upper branches: skeletons of old umbrellas
draped with dyed fabrics. Even here under
fluorescents the cast shadows spell labor
and grief, the tints of joy, stories of fathers
taken away, the legends of indigo.
                    Across the room, across
the sacred grove's hardwood forest floor,
dyeing pots hidden by trees in Arianne's
"The Music of Osun," the Yoruba river goddess
with her eyes closed, her moon face risen

into the color of yams, a woman dancing,
her braids swinging free of Detroit, of history
untelling itself in the Sea Islands, before cotton,
sugar, tobacco,
        Arianne dancing at the goddess's edge,
on feathery tips of indigo, Oshogbo and Yoruba
the wind's praise, fertile syllables, each morning
a lost princess rising from the water, brass bangles
along her arms, her fingers blue, Arianne singing.

MOON

Ring

Hugged gravity of the gibbous moon,
this perfect circle, a chipped white plate

its center, a pale reach the compass leg
inscribing silvery thought, red to violet,

surrounding bow. How is the world,
broken, turning in stillness, not moon?

Rising

So large! The tide roiling, the sea-wound
and broil like a dream afraid, the moon

so near. A pale basket being hauled
into the sky, beginning a separation,

the amazed heart swelling; a redness
failing in the west; our breath caught up.

Full

What I carry with me from the North
fallen into a glittering field

of sea, the water's many small deaths
the timid openings of memory.

Whatever I was, whoever you
are, dolor of ghostly origins

all around us, this stripping off, this
pallor as we step out of our names.

CROSSING THE FOLLY

1

Spotlight trained up into this palmetto's
frond head—sudden wild hair crackling
silvery as moonlight sliding along ocean.
By morning, wet lumpy sand; armatures
of broken whelk; crab-death; on their parchment
backs, humped, tailed horseshoes; tucked-up
jointed legs in moon-snail shell—dubious
hermits out of prayer and patience among
tangled ivory egg-cases trailed in tide,
inbreeding, inseeming, inuring not long enough.
The palmetto leans toward wind and the clean
blue light coming off-sea: wrapped in horny
dead-lace, shedding below itself gravity
of purpose: tall trunk texture near in surface
to the roughened tail of the opossum; callused
extremity, insight that does no further good—
to sway from heights, rooted unrecompensed
until its wind-blown berries begin to fall.

2

I leave the spider crab on its back
as the sea withdraws, many small
appendages digging among miniscule
coquinas and broken cockles.
The purple sea-whip a thin animal
because it hungers for its own and leaves
a history in a filigree of nerves that is

like a branch dragging on the ground.
The pelican circles like an eagle,
the marsh fills from the sea,
small things burrow deep that have no bone
or iridescent shell risen from soft digestive parts.
The sun lowering into a purple abyss
because I toss a beached crayfish back
into the tide and wonder what external
skeleton I need to bear the weight of nothingness.

3

The tide flowing out of the marsh into this channel,
cow-lick terns exhausted from twisting down through
the air for menhaden. Now I walk the littoral all
the way to Port Royal, step over protruded tubes
of clam worms, the sea dreaming only of itself,
while the salts of rivers pour into its watery mind
a narrative of cities. I can go and return. One-legged
willets in tidal pools probing their own images for
souls. The Hotel Westin, the Pelican Bar, live swans
preening on meshed-in ponds; wet heron sculptures
long-necked in a quest that has petrified. These
carpeted paths the turns into pleasantry; boardwalk,
deck; dank rows of cushioned chaise longues;
the rusted echo of summer in empty drink holders
screwed to the arms of chairs. My time here limited,
anxious, as the moon shrugs off the sea. The Folly
filled with bream. The littoral flooding toward green
panic grass; tumbling into salt the sandspur's spiny
burrs that cling to shoes, transporting them across
the dunes. Me the prickly ambassador of the other side.

Sept. 14, something trailing us from New York, smoke, odor of
      burnt
flesh, noise of jet engines seen in billows of flames, heard in the
      dark
retina of memory, something behind us like crowded parking lots
in train stations, no drivers returning to drive back home, a bitter
taste like the urine of someone else's God, people nodding at our

NY license plates where we stop for gas, Maryland, Virginia, the
Carolinas, as if we'd driven from the front, our cats and
      belongings
piled into an old ambulance, no sly glance at northerners or hoot
and guffaw at snow birds. Respect and sadness. Heads shaking
back and forth, Who can believe it? We have come here empty-

handed, without flowers or the veil of grief, our little house back
home being renovated, gutted, slabs of granite hoisted onto
      cabinets,
ceilings torn away, smoke detectors with eerie green lights
      throbbing
in freshly cut halls. All that stainless steel gathering heat and chill,
black gratings that mask the touch of hunger, their gleam of

darkness congealed; the floors, the beautiful hardwood floors
elongating the grain of oak and cherry, where we'll walk in bare
feet in the first land's bounty, never thinking to feel so fortunate
as we feel here along the lagoon, renting relief from icy paths,
startled by a golden eagle landing in the backyard, his talons

curved on nothing, until he rises briefly to the railing of the deck,
eyeing the small movements that enticed him out of his glide
over the marshland. Now he lunges and rises again, something
in his grip, hanging helplessly, not dead, not alive, the gray color
of a northern sky, sides heaving, carried toward the highest pine.

DREAM

The apartment house we lived in burned down to the second story, blackened timbers smoking. The bed I slept in a crumble of cinders; the double bed where my father read cheap detective novels now a warped mattress spring, wooden slats consumed, everything soft or sentimental melted away. Across the absence somehow the remains of the other bedroom survive, a narrow bed for my mother sleeping apart, the bureau in which I shared a drawer, outlines of the single closet; the wire hangers for her aprons whose pockets she filled with raw carrots. I hear the sound of her eating them late at night. The doorway of that time like a furrow dolphins make, a depth surmised. Continuance believed in.

OUTSIDER ART

Or visionary. Or raw. Primitive.
Naif. As if being abandoned in a corn field
at birth, a child of the veil, caul
over her face, weren't enough to send a woman
to the easel. Except there is no easel. No
canvas. Only a door. So she paints on the door.
"The Devil Have Folks Coming Out His Ears,
Eyes, Mouth and Butt." A deaf man leans
toward red geraniums blooming just before a frost
and he scolds them, "You fools!" Another
paints with mud and molasses—showing
the wealthy the true nature of their homes
on plaster board that they hang in their
parlors. Here's the piano cow with ivory keys
along her spine. A gray-haired Mary holding
the dead Christ, painted on the lid of a flour
drum. Who has ever seen her in her age? An old man's
face on dented rusted tin has his own kind
of crumpled truth. There was a man who painted
his sofa, his floor, his lamp shades, toilet tank,
visions pouring out of his long brush.
It arrives any time of life. The seeing.
The feel that is texture. The bright pinks
and greens of a fractured dawn, the dewless
smooth petals, the voice in the tree, where twin
peacocks face each other, "You will bloom forever."

WATCHING THE MEDIEVAL MYSTERY PLAYS
AND THINKING OF MILTON

Performed by a South African troupe
at the Spoleto Festival

Lucifer is speaking Xhosa, Afrikaans, English; the hell
mouth of one self-begot; flames escaping the open
stage floor. In the galley above, Raphael explaining
fallen brightness should consider itself less than
perfection; evil the loss of degree, the failure of
patience. The man next to me reeking of after-shave,
golden chain around his neck; his 60+ years a flaw
in hotel mirrors: astringent unguents the distilled
memory of Eden. He's suffocating us. A sweet raw
chemical tracking through our lungs, upending
taste, a mineral heaviness in our words, until
later in the warm air of Charleston, meanings fall
unprovoked from us, unimplored, the grace of evening
filtering down from stars that burned out so long ago.

NEWS FROM HOME

Our daughter is trying to have a baby.
My brother, who watched from the 19th story
of his building, still dreams of people leaping
out of the Tower's windows, floor collapsing
upon floor, the sun a zinc penny in the rancid
sky. The snow is falling like loosening fleece.
Our daughter is speaking to her body,
"crocus, forsythia, tulip, azalea, baby's breath."
She says Sal our contractor is chipping ice off
the rear patio, drilling an arm-size hole in the
brick wall for the dryer's vent. The wind still blows
dust over the river, my brother's face gray in his mirror.
The new mail box is green on a cream-colored post.
She says the mail carrier left the box of our chocolates
at the kitchen door and it lay buried for two days.
She says she is trying to persuade those narrow
tubes that her eggs need space and safe passage.
The Norway spruce and Douglas firs are swaying
like elevator shafts. Deer are eating the rhododendrons,
green-stained lips are sealing the envelopes that
forward our mail. The snow has been plowed
to one side by a man with one arm. The crack
maple has cracked, the fox has torn open last
night's compost bag before it got to the compost pit,
the dawn breaks over the reservoir like spilled
light before it hardens, the spinning at night is
the Fraioli girl's bald tires, my brother still wakes
at night on the fourth floor of his co-op building,
heat pressing at the window. Snow is still falling.
Our daughter is trying to have a baby.

REFLECTIONS

A great blue heron standing at lagoon's
edge, his twin shimmering upside-down,
feet rippling, another long neck and glistening
eye, head cocked to one side, his slicked-back crest
where he's fallen away. He's split off a second
self, and where he steps slowly in the shallows,
rearranging the spilled white streak
of his head, his hunched shoulders shattering
beneath him, I look down from the bridge
to see a white-haired man rising to the surface.

The question is how the leaf-littered current
flows while upside-down firs and live oaks
hold steady. Or if the motionless blue heron
keeps the glitter of his eye fixed on the oily
stillness of a watery surface just because
something of him is looking upwards into
sky. Brown pine needles float past. A faint
chipping of birds breaks off bits of air
as if it were a brittle thing. This is memory
making itself available. This is the shaking
of a friend's hand bringing a spoon to his mouth.
This is the song trapped in his wife's mind
because she can no longer speak, while moss
hangs from a tree, swaying above itself
in the unfiltered shadow that ripples
without a sound toward the sluiced sea.

TRIO

1

PLANTATION

Middleton Place

Tree bigger than Whitman's live oak lonely
as himself in a furnished room, here in the unknown
years before an Englishman came upriver with
shackled slaves. Tree thick with indifference
at the edge of camellia allées, gnarled ascent
clutched by resurrection fern above the rice
fields once an unflooded earth before seeds
for partridge berry or trillium or violets
ferried across an ocean became the hoards
dying in torrid summer. Tree before hoe,
harrow, flail, roots humped like workers
rising with their backs to the sun, the crepe
myrtle only recently big, now two hedges further
from incessant shade. Tree before "agrarian,"
"parterre," "malaria," "leisurely spirit"
the whip of an age, before aproned dark women
bury a brass-edged leather trunk in the terraced
garden, tucking away the miniature portrait
of Washington, his high collar tattered
as Confederate dollars and the gilt-framed
lagoons of Venice wrapped in drapes from Belgium—
a row of slave houses no longer crowded with prayer,
lives twisting into yarn, suddenly a voided
grief, while raucous Union troops pour
off boats on the Ashley River, their oiled
torches blooming in late morning to stifle
the cool composure of vast rooms with blue flame.

2

MUSEUM

Savannah

The art pretty poor. Faded, splotched statues with broken
genitals. Tall portrait of a poet simpering down on us with pity
because we're out of step, our words don't scan. But a few
     original
sculptures—two swans twisting their necks into a lover's braid.
Calder's girl scratching her foot. On the first floor, behind the
     stairs,
a bronze Russian mother clasps her child in 1927, ten years after
the Revolution, the mobbed streets, the smoke. There's a gap
in the chocolate cornice on the south wall, where another wall
separated violent voices, something seditious ceded from the heart,
pocket doors closed on argument; servants rushed away
with the best porcelain. In a niche that was the velvet space
around a Ming vase, a redframed window opens on the city's
quaintest square. Unemployed black men light up, lounging
on benches. Gawking strangers roll past in tourist trolleys.
Everywhere a dark light plugged in the mouths of cannons.
Another period room. Scenes on blockprinted wallpaper
repeat themselves—the same cathedral again, again. A pinched
liturgy of towers, clouds twinning themselves, a river, a tradition
feeding on itself, evenly flowing through faint seams, a boatman
and his doubles poling their way toward an esplanade, all these
     ladies
ballooning in the same dresses, waiting with insipid eyes, as if un-
comprehending that wherever they turn, they see themselves
and all of us, the stained mirror in its gilt Rococo frame
returning the one scene upon frilled scene, the one time only.
More than a hundred years ago, General Sherman requisitioned

the grille-worked home down the street. His men billeted them-
    selves
and horses in the cemetery, removing the now blurred tombstones,
propped them along a wall. Names lifted and leaning away from
their bones. Standing for anonymous earth. For silent dustless
gleam in a museum hall and pastoral drapes that shut out war.

3

EXCAVATION

Folly Island

Dig a shallow trench, *"To take as it ware our*
Lives in our Hands." What tide there was yet eats
the shore, nudging the skeletons without skulls
or the long bones of the hand or the taste of
cherry bounce, sago, rum. Typhoid fever leaves
little to speak of. They didn't say much,
settling like center muck in barrels buried
to make wells, a song crumbling in the wind
beneath swaying moss. Carved bullets and tin
buttons still rise to the surface. The leather
forage straps rotted from their caps recently
unbuckled in haste, left on the dank sand,
the tales of their African fathers interred like
grommets from their rubber ponchos. Dead white
officers disbelieved their skills. In this air,
bright flutter of the unit's "F," a brigade
of voices, tattered friends, where the body turns
toward Charleston and the murmur of ghostly guns.

"YOU AIN'T HURRYIN' ME"

On a house tour, tapping my foot to a bluegrass band,
eating fried chicken at Mackay Point Plantation. The banjo
player looks like a winter tourist in sandals, wearing sunglasses,
strumming a poem, the snow of South Dakota fallen from
his hair; the tall skinny woman playing bass, eyes squinched,
is Mrs.Vogel, who taught me geometry, how triangles
might bulge in a round world, tangling me in proofs,
even here, where Robert E. Lee came away with "Traveler,"
the horse who pawed the air at Gettysburg. I'm looking
at the Pocotaglio, Tulifinny and Coosawhatchie Rivers
mixing three watery legs of a history that nothing
in the Bible would make equal in all its sides to the slave
labor that planted these allées of live oaks. That cleared
the land before the hurricanes and the boll weevil made all
of this a nowhere that bluegrass thumping fills to the brim.

READING CZESLAW MILOSZ

"I speak to you with silence like a cloud or a tree"

The acid air of burn-off in Bluffton
drifts over the lagoon, incinerated husks
and grass turning rich blackness into
the history of earth. Your Warsaw's ruins
embering in the breath of exhausted oak
leaves, the clog of streets, gutters flaring
as vibrancy rises here, the narrow
sapling a splintered doorjamb, a child's face
the bud unfolding scrape of azaleas.
Gray fume is spreading the history
of bones, books in rubble, their charred titles
crumbling like dirt from the shoes of workers.
A sour after-taste blows out to sea,
the salt world turning on itself, griefless
ground at zero another drowned abyss.
Resort workers are planting zinnias, roots
smothered in red mulch, orange heads, burst suns,
buried lives again giving up their heat.

LEAVING HOME

2002

Thule carrier strapped to the roof rack.
Cats in their cages. Computer covered
in black plastic, a packaged silence. I'm
scraping the windshield, the road already
rumbling in my hand, its slush and broken
pavement tumbling toward us from a future
we will outrun. What do we need? One change
of clothes. Tolls for exits. The long single
bridge in our minds assembled from segments
that span the fogged valleys and the many
rivers we must cross. Something happening
to our speech, a stillness between us like
patience: the long breath of a tidal dawn
bringing washed-up reeds, a wavering line of
pelicans crossing the still visible moon.

SINGLETON BEACH

Dolphins in the ebb-tide shallows
break the surface from such
a marginal depth they must be
scraping the harbor bottom
that is constantly changing—
sand and small debris migrated
here from somewhere like Portugal,
long traveled, land to land across
an ocean, the taste foreign, lips
staggered with nouns, nibble and
verb, a kind of speech. And what
are you, crunching along strewn,
vacated shells, frightening willets, year-
old gulls, not even sandpipers tolerating
your approach as they throw themselves
into the air? The tide curls back a tumble
of horseshoe shelters, trilobites pre-historic,
the finger sponge torn from invisible grasp,
its time arbitrary, coquinas flashing color.
Everything rising to be seen and thrown
out of its element into transformation,
the moon mind almost ascending, dusk,
death, dearth that hums into the bone,
this, then, the gleam of your turning
and going back, footprints washed away.

BOUNDARIES

The poem unbounded and believed, risen from a sandy soil and left to the hands of nieces and nephews without a word written down.

Just "this ancient shell ring." "That wax myrtle." "The crooked live oak." "All the land between."

The poem within that scrapes itself on the thatched bark of a young palmetto as it tries to extricate itself.

A young girl still wet from Skull Creek toweling her hair in the yard that her family has sat in since the first Union troops wrote home about malaria and marsh. About the dry-throated call of the great blue heron gliding out of its solitude.

Out of the poem.

DREAM

They stab into the tray of sunflower seeds—a downy woodpecker, titmice with black dot eyes, jittery chickadees, a blackbird shrieking "raw! raw!" Kinglets so small the neighborhood hawk swallows them whole. This flitter a tremble of lagoon, I'm on it, floating face up. The snake bird's yard-long neck, like a loose cord in the water beneath me, tightens suddenly, her lunge rippling through lungs and heart. What do I remember? Another compass time, the shadow falling, a weathered lattice separating caution from the ragged smell of animals. Lesser paw prints on the kitchen window, the compost bag torn apart, all that inedible rind and dusk—the milk bone thrown to the giant hound that slavers in the woods. A quiet snowfall softening detail, powdering to the touch.

IN THE GULLAH FLEA MARKET

Rainy day. I'm going out on route 278,
turning left at Squire Pope Road, where
lookouts in trees once scanned Port Royal
Sound for Union ships. I'm parking, walking
past wet bicycles tagged at $75, their miles
metallic with odors of fatback and collards
beginning to ferment. Inside, tripping over
vacuum cleaners without wheels, I've bonked an
elbow on small-screen TVs peering blindly
in the echo of pratfalls, sitcom gags slackened
out of their time, fathers in business suits
halloing into a dark hall, snow drifting

across the hours, into the aisle where I've
picked up lint from chenille bedspreads
stuffed into a sleep of twenty years. The
Nigerian vendor behind trays of bracelets
and carved bone earrings stands to rearrange
Ghanian coin masks that hang with tarnished
currency, smudged profiles of heroes, the sharp-
nosed Queen; the vacancy of wealth obvious
in papier-maché eye sockets, a coarse cinder-block
wall, the moldering of empire, while I back into
prongs of a barbecue fork, jostle piles of crescent
wrenches, lock-jaw pliers biting uselessly into air.

A *TV Guide* slips off its 1980 stack, opening
to programs I must have seen, my mother in ICU,
the flexible tube of the respirator in her mouth,

her eyes searching, looking toward the grimy
blinds of a window and the wall that opens beyond.
I'm here among rotted spines of arithmetic
books signed on the title page by sixth-graders
with a flourish toward fame. An old Remington
half-revealed in its stained case like the one
I hocked to pay the rent, going for weeks in long-
hand on East Sixth Street, salsa pulsing the walls
as I lift the maple top of the TV/stereo combo and
spin the turntable with a 45-rpm adapter slipped
down the spindle like a tourniquet to slow

the rhythm of need, while the young couple
behind me grows bored with watching such dim
progress among pink Depression glass and green
chipped pitchers that someone poured lemonade
from in 1948 after a scorching day delivering
laundry. But there's no cord to plug into this
bulbous chrome percolator. No way to warm
the last drop. Or sweep away the scurf of dried-out
foam rubber cushions that kept me upright
when I drew diagrams for Mr. Jablonsky's science
class, made black-ink drawings of Erlenmeyer
flasks. I'm standing here among dusty bone
china, running my finger along an edgy whiteness,
the lost heat of a future.

OUTLET MALL

Come here when the sea-fog rolls to the door
and the sky's gray bed sheet slips down over
the terrace view. Take the bridge over Skull
Creek and Pinkney Island's prickly oyster sill
to the mainland and this place where white-haired men
with stiff knees walk in jogging suits next to women
who tirelessly seek a marked-down crystal flute
from Ireland or Dan River sheets like the marsh at
sunset, reduced to a few fuchsia rays that almost
bring color to your eyes. Try on the hooded coat
with toggles that don't quite interlock, because
in her last hour on the line, the worn Chinese
woman making it was thinking of her feverish child.
These brands have laces too long, one instep twisted
out of stride, a seam that runs down the world spine
suited to curvatures of the calcium poor, a jagged line
of straight pins to stab vanity.

READING TENNESSEE WILLIAMS

Not his plays. His poems. The word
"loneliness" enabling as a wing feather
on this yearling gull ambling past, speckled,
solitary, until he takes flight. I flip
the page into a New Orleans brothel,
genital sorrow. Relief. That mottled
gull now further down the beach,
sitting in a tidal pool, fluffing his wings.

A footnote on the house in Key
West: Tennessee's gazebo of commemoration,
the plaques he hung for the loved
and lost, the obsessive rose
that can only be itself in slow humid
evenings. Why do lovers sit up anxious
about the dawn? That gull leaving
its shimmering pool, solitude

now grace in air, riding a thermal toward
Tybee Island. What does it matter
that love and terror meet in ordinary
rhyme, if the current where wing
insinuates itself is the shape of glory
and remembrance, the wind's deceit
a charmed accent that beguiles
soaring youth forever disdaining to land?

PRESERVE

That it should inhere beyond cut
pines, uprooted shrubs, a willfullness dug
through the soft needled floor of flat
woods, someone has set aside her other
balance sheet and bequeathed the pond,
the low ground called *pocasin* by first inhabitants
who knew the smooth leaves on Dahoon holly
and in their bad time gathered gallberry,
chainfern, fetterbush, where a bald cypress
exposes polished knees like someone used
to kneeling. Anxiety and weariness shed
in this place of longneedled pines, their
cones like bristling planets above our
heads. The pond's shifting green
stain is the motion of the elastic sides
of water, hands held in the air as if
new in their skin; crushed scent of verdant
world the taste beneath tongue, our senses
born in the shadows of cherry laurel and
sassafras, the sun beating through the dust
that has left such a grayness over face and eyes.

SCENES FROM THE PASSING WORLD

Remember those Japanese prints and the tale of pines
who softened down their length to become human?
Even if we wore the ceramic masks of an aged
couple crossing the creek in sudden rain,

    the same rain beating down on the old rice fields
    all over Jasper County,

by morning you'd be the girl holding her loose sleeve
to her face, while I read from a scroll of plum blossoms,

    promising rejuvenation, describing this beach, this littoral,
    these washed-up leopard crabs snipping the air to right
    themselves,

the tangle of whelk egg casing an interior thrown
clear, each pin-prick hole a birth toward hardness
drawn from the sea,

    a dim light moving like the brush of an
    artist mourning the pleasure districts
    passing from the memory of his city,

time and the narrow bridge over Broad River
the spans that grayness begets of gray,

    the antebellum silence of old homes
    in Beaufort the humid intake of an unjust age
    and the sweet crumbling of a luncheon cake,

this moment given for walking through the cast-
up swash line into early evening, dried spartina
crackling beneath our step,

loss and waste washing into the sea, pelicans
gliding out of fog, their faces shaped to a long hunger.

2003

*Driven or drawn, the last leaves, the long falling
pine needles that will be golden straw: we're in
the mix of history and place, the burlap-wrapped
Japanese maple already thinning down its eastern
side. Just look at the miles on our Taurus wagon,
the dink in the passenger door. The flicker of that
red Aladdin's lamp in the dash display, when oil
pressure weakens. We're fixed and ready, polity
freezing over, my hands stiffening inside gloves
that somewhere else, in a desert, are crusted with
sand, the night's artillery like the cracking of ice
in trees.*

A BROKEN STAIR

Out in the lagoon this morning, the snowy
egret striding in the shallow brown water
has nothing to do except wade and think,
the budding azaleas open, bleeding
all morning—this day we hear Ruth Ann
has died, this time of the egret making
its way on rich silt. Where is it friends go
on a black slippery road, leaving covers
twisted in their unmade beds, such hurry
they're in to be gone? Her words went
with her. A half-emptiness that she couldn't
swallow left in her glass of water, the faint
music of her presence in the hall, children's
"hello? hello?" a hiss on the dangling phone.

We're pushing down the stiff door latch,
stepping out into morning, looking down
the worn porch stairs, the board of a riser
hanging loose, nails pulled free. Falling
here would be so easy, so much ground
rising to meet us, smeary crushed palmetto
berries the stain of a future. And as I pound
the board back in place, the small muscles
in my hand cramping mid-sentence, titmouse,
cardinal, nuthatch sharing a scatter of seed
beneath the feeder, why are the vibrations
up and down the stair like tremors in an
extended hand, a cup of tea rattling—
its pale sound that of a bird wading?

THE SIGHTING

Perhaps it *is* an indigo bunting with bluish
head and wings. Noisy families come up flushed
from the beach, stomping sand from their feet.
Both of us amazed by the bird, another and
another, extricating themselves from waxy
myrtle. That flash of color like a dye
across the afternoon, opening and closing,
a fabric torn asunder, then settling,
until the breeze opens it again, a wound.
Perhaps it *isn't* an indigo bunting with bluish
back, the color of its head and wings an after-
image in our minds, which foist among
the waxy myrtle a flutter of rags, the noisy
families tramping onto the walkway from
the beach just bruising a stillness in the air.
It *could* be an indigo bunting with bluish
eyes, with so much art in the being of being.
A way of tilting wings so that the budding
myrtle seems a fragrance dizzying the birds.
Those families shaking the drift of mountains
from their feet, an erosion of heights, abhorring
what has been carried on the wind for years
and years in the voice of greenness.

DE BLUE KEEPS D'EM HAINTS AWAY

*"Creatures of the night won't pass through openings
painted heaven blue."*
                              On mirrors designed by Marci Tressel

The tide turns silver and they soar toward the moon
like the abrupt heron as he lifts his long frame into
the mystery not even *his* eyes can pierce, for blue
has washed down his hunched shoulders from the
dark of his mind, his landing irritable and awkward
just where the marsh is soft enough to be impressed
by him. Each hour a misted mirror, a blue border
around all your seeing. How easily mood detaches
itself, the end feathers of a bird left in the teeth of

something quick and fierce. These mirrors on the
gallery wall like portals, in each one the faces
that imitate sleep. You can see the boyhood river,
the city park, the haunted meals of the homeless
brother who left no word, carefully contained
by the writing on a frame. Blueshifted sky lowering
to the pond's shimmer, nothing not snatched away
or flown back into the mouthshaped shadows trying
to speak as the heron steers himself on the all-carrying air.

CONSTRUCTION

They're ripping out palmettos and myrtle across
the street, flattening the land, bulldozing gritty soil.
Another house. The dumpster in front emits growls
and chirps, something scratching. It's raccoons
scuttling under shattered 2X4's, caught in the intricate
tunnels of broken glass, plastic bags, chunks of concrete,
styrofoam cups, branches broken from beneath the feet
of cedar waxwings, the quiet ooze of beer cans. Voices
ping like sonar, and the security guard we called
is smacking his lips, hand on his holstered weapon.
"They'll get out. They got in there, didn't they?"

Those people went to their 9-to5 jobs a little early,
without breakfast. Suddenly, coffee cups trembled
and a wall caved in. Flames slashed through the floor,
the ceiling gone, a vacuum opening its portal, the song
of nothingness the only lyric outside and inside,
a long ashy field that is memory blown toward the
harbor. Heavy equipment later digging up layers,
fume, stench, blood boiled away. In another city now
a screech shatters the sky. Children are trapped
under debris. Tanks pound the broken pavement.

Perhaps he was right. By noon, the dumpster quiet.
I'm writing on a pad, the dock slanted beneath me,
two stanchions eaten through, the lagoon turbid,
rippling. I wish I were clear-headed. I wish I had
seen the raccoons running off, hunched, bear-like,
the small imitating the large, this breeze not carrying

such stink of diesel trucks, this South by the Sea peeling
off a stained brochure. What I remember of loss
a scant rubble beneath a thin tower of words, my sister's
suicide face, our father's unheard moan somewhere
in the unbelieving air.

ENTRIES

Sinistral

Accreted darkness, this whelk's gate of glossed
sea-breath, in its twistings a life
that slides away from rhetoric and spongy
closure, stranded at the swash line
of desiccated marsh grass, dry cores
clotted with grains that have glittered
down the years from wind-worn mountain
Appalachia for miles and miles, while
the copper-heavy minds of horseshoe crabs
drain into night. Something caused this creature
to turn away, to extrude a different winding—
left-curved, left-sounding. Now it has died.
In moonlight, ghost crabs amble out of
burrows, sideways clacking over elegant disks,
over jingle shells, over moon-snail-drilled
housing once a flow of chalky sea that
provides every visible means.

Dextral

This whelk shell a helio-fated open-
mouthed singer; the turns in its throat
the sudden unconscious movements
of a voice veering into desire's edge.
In its vocabulary of egg casings,
a society—this broken parchment, this
pouring out of miniscule whelks into

my open palm, a bright slope inward
and visible on their right-turning spiral:
showing a history in the moral of mica grains
dotted with penny wort, chips of barnacled
wood, open-slit olive shell inscribed
with sea script, pioneering grasses
migrating beyond dunes. The saw palmetto
shedding its berries, and by midnight newly
hatched turtles flopping toward the moonlit sea.

DREAM

My gloved hand holding a long icicle. Then a bird's wing, the bird fluttering madly. It's a dove. I let it go and turn on my side, as if dreaming. But there's no bed. No lamp. No you. What am I lying on? Pages and pages of it. Here's a sentence just in from the north, its milky breath clouding my face, its eyes bright. Hey! A cold hand down the back of my shirt. Out the window, I see the golf course on fire across the street. The long-billed ibises are burning. Snowy egrets fill the smoldering trees. You are next to me, your hand in mine, everything beautiful, a crimson sun, the live oak toppling. Don't cry, don't cry!

READING MARIANNE MOORE

" . . . *it is human nature to stand in the middle of a thing,
but you cannot stand in the middle of this. . . .* "

Revetment, sea wall, groin, there's no end to saving
a beach: dredging sea-bottom sand accumulated
in the southward drift from Port Royal to Land's
End; maybe bits of drowned history, all the large
shatter of cockles and crab, Indian pottery
shards, a buckle, Confederate cap rotted free
of rebel yells: churned through chutes into a barge,
    into an idea of permanence. As if the Marriott

would not one day slide into a sea *looking
as if it were not that ocean in which dropped
things are bound to sink.* Still, keeping it still,
a life-long holding in one place—the school books
strapped together by father's old belt, the kitchen
of childhood Wheaties, the slow wash of memory
trapped in a glass. The morning walks you and I took
    on this surface yet inherent in its slipping away,

from Folly Beach to South Beach, from sea walls and sea
roaches that eat flotsam to sea sponges and fecal
pellets of sand shrimp, thing to thing, with room for
pangolin, paper nautilus, camel sparrow,
if such *models of exactness* come to mind,
neither tactile nor visible, our own unweariness
spiting erosion, pulsation, noise that
    batters *neither with volition nor consciousness.*

RAPTURE

After paintings by Donna Howells

In certain paintings, people disappear
while reading menus in brightly lit diners,
empty sweaters, vacated jeans, sagged-
out, often-washed shirts littering the
floor, but laid out as neatly as children's
summer camp clothes folded by their
mother on a bed. You see some of these
stripped people rising in the sky, almost
colliding with hawks, and down below
there's the Church of the Luke Warm
with its narrow driveway the color of
bad peaches, parents on their knees in the
withered grass, holding up their hands
in grief, where the little socks and sneakers

lie abandoned. Look out for the sky-borne
elderly trailing long white hair, or the
helicopter tilting to avoid the flash of so
much skin, the whirring blades, the beaten
air, the sermon bulging its way through
half-open windows. I tell you this because
I fainted once in church, a warm April
morning, I fell back against the people
behind me, I never touched the ground.
Today, walking the beach, I'm buttoned
and zipped, my photo-gray glasses grow
darker in the sun, while sea crows and grackles
mock each other in the pines. Listen.
And don't tell me you know anything.

Sonogram: two girls curled upon themselves.
One touches her lips as if to speak. The other
shadow, her sister, drifts behind, already
not listening. Our daughter's daughters in
their mother sea half-luminous, half-dark,
photographed, disturbed, the reverse thrum
and tide that lifts and lowers them the way
world welcomes with intrusion, interference,
goggling eyes. Now would be the time to tell them
what they share with dolphins and soft-bellied
spirits listening just below the surface
of light. Here, so far south, their grandfather
lifts his eyes to the stark glimmer of rising
sun, a russet beach, such amazement as brings
time by the handful and the sifting hour
pours golden, gritty with eons, the promise
of birds named in flight, pelican, ring-billed
gull, arctic tern, the ice glitter and ocean
foam, or tumbled carapace or fading moon
an inheritance it will take years to explain.

Traffic, so much of it in our lives. Comings.
Goings. Silent sentences in airwaves. The plow
we're behind shoving new snow and dirty
crusts of last week's fall. Maybe south is only sweat,
spotted windshield, pine straw caught in blades,
Spanish moss falling from a height, where the snake
bird curls her impossible swallowing in the live oak.
Maybe this wide-eyed, half-sobbing sound of our
engine is what it means to feel the vernal equinox
while asleep, the windows of Hampton Inn shuddering
in the wake of trucks, the flea-market trailers with
***Florida** painted in green, the dry call of the boat-*
tailed grackle what I thought a sore throat, half-speech,
our bleared hesitation passing the diesel-fume plow
just a kind of breathing out, before we inhale what
animals know of fear and the hunger that never dies.

Well, Plato. And Whitman. Or Bacon, "a very scanty
regard paid to invisible things." On a deck chair facing
the ocean, all this shimmer and drip-inherent substance
where attention is always dissolving, I think of the night
beach: hispid cotton rats snuffling for seed among the dunes,
deer browsing sea oats, the name sliding off its thing
      (things detached from us ... there is no end of thought ...),
the waste pellets seeping to the surface from ghost shrimp
six feet below. The big-eyed beach fleas really crustaceans,
who can hear the snip of their miniscule claws, amid all those
that anchor, crawl or burrow?
      A doorway of little facts, seething.
Take the sea hares, snails without shells. I can feel their softness
swollen with moon-pull, a slithering roundness, even as I think
Fallujah. Baghdad. The waist strapped with explosives.
    Mourners
lifted to the heavens on concussive hate. The boy from Iowa now
looking, now not,
    then the space where the face has gone and the gaze remains.
       By what history shall we know ourselves? East
of here, in the marsh, the black needle rush grows waist high,
its hollow, sharp-pointed stems tinted dusty gray, the succulent
glasswort reddish green, only 5 inches toward the sun, why should
the flicker and hermit thrush cross each other's paths in the same
moment as a word falters, this cold fire of singleness almost
an afflicted
    wing of singed bits made of the glances that reach it?

WATCHING WEATHER

It's easier than saving a stranded loon,
her leg broken, where she scrambles
away from high tide, and the whole range
of us walks by. "She's done for." "Call wild-life
rescue." "She's a cormorant." It's appraisal
and north always roiling before the eyes
like the villagers gone mad, banging
the metal light poles with rocks, warning
everyone what's to come. Or who.
The shore line a hundred years ago
farther out than we walk each morning.
A lost limit like snow flakes dissolving
at first touch and remembered crossing into
the Carolinas. This heat, my love, the reason
the world sinks beneath us and we change
channels. We extrapolate. We shed. Think
the past and it rises to meet us. The heron
lifting himself into jasmine-scented air.
A thought spreads buoyantly invisible as the
breath of fasting saints, foul, intransigent,
that neither of us inhales forever. Snow
spreading across a TV screen. The lake effect
causeless as the kiss of a stranger.

IN THE FOREST

Black-and-white young Matthew, his instinct
to take the high ground driving him halfway up
the spiral staircase to the loft. *Cat Ascending.*
Sun blazing in the Palladian window like something
out of William Blake. This energy of *Tiger, Tiger*
a fierce impress upon Matthew's pupils that are
contracting even as he crouches, ready to leap
onto the window cornice, that ledge his predator's
heart lunges to achieve, with what dread feet,
to what aspire, amid the unwiped dust, attached
wooden blinds that come crashing to the carpeted floor
like a rotted limb falling in forest mulch. I wake
that night, my pulse palpable, beating at my ears.
Say, then, we never left that place. The names we
gave to fruit, bush, tree, flower, beast and fowl
fell away, each thing new to itself, shadows in
moonlight nothing but memory they cast away,
the wind scraping palmetto fronds, eager
lover, transparent fingers that let the body show
through, where caress and secret grasp will bleed,
thorns acquire, the soft movement all around us
triggering the sensor and outdoor lights, Matthew
rushing to his window to watch the parting of myrtle,
camellia, the forgetful emptiness that is brushing past.

DREAM

I'm reading Milosz in a bombed-out building. A half-wall faces east, behind me another one crumbling, about to fall, a hanged man swinging on the gallows, but it's no one I know. I'm turning pages in the dust-clouded air, useless 1939 barrage balloons fallen, flat as dead lungs, even though as I read I know I can't, because no one reads in dreams, that part of the brain elsewhere, pleasing only itself. Sudden wind, the Muse is trying to cross her legs in the back of the Trireme, her veils aflutter, the three banks of oars dipping and rising suddenly on Broad Creek, the pluff mud beginning to show as the tide oozes back into Calibogue Sound. Out of my time, out of my place, the wrong war, an ageless crooning in the sky, a rotating artillery shell, the *crawk* of a great blue heron the crackle in a poor man's hearing. The bib under my chin, stained with barbecue drippings, I've ripped it off to read its embroidered *Happy Father's Day*, but I can't make sense of it. What brings the day? Your hand in mine, our friends backing out of the driveway, headed home to Key West. We wave. Pampas grass suddenly in my face, I'm looking through to the sea. Three coast guard helicopters thud-thudding overhead.

TWINS

New and small, seeing little of the dark Unknowing
you shared, your raised arms and eyes not so unalike as to
blur sisterhood, each yourself alone, yet curled hair
and frown the ancestral residue of someone gone before—
a great aunt's quarrel with herself still echoing within,

a door opening on the Aegean, father's stone-bruised
hands like his father's at the nets, land and sea the soft clash
of inheritance. A nurse is lowering you, Katherine, into my
daughter your mother's arms, and Viktoria clings, her grip
a protest demanding sister near, side by side remembered.

Perhaps one of you will always find a latch to press. The other
will see doors in clouds—a kind of flight she must forsake
for the hard ground that seed splits upon. Down here the
blaze of spirit, and pain, stark as broken glass, so years
to come take in your sisterly arms each other's need,

watch the great blue heron soar. We're part creature, part cloud,
ethereal interior of bone; the light that flashes through thought,
where vase and the vase itself collide. The slow tide rising to
scrawl the salt future is just the moon. How long before you
are all arms and outcry, clomping in mother's shoes outside my door?

CRIME REPORT

A cell phone, a voice still explaining debt,
and a watch not quite ticking but valued at
$150 have been stolen from a Tahoe outside
a home on _____ O Court. Jewelry valued
at $550 and electronics at $330 lifted from
a house along Long Cove, the boat rocking
quietly where there's no tide. An all-terrain
vehicle of undisclosed make valued at $8,232
pinched from Bluffton House apartments, where
Simmonsville Rd. empties frighteningly into
Rte. 278 (otherwise called Fording Island
Rd.). The passenger's side window, windshield
and headlight of a dump truck and two windows
on an excavator broken at a construction site
on Baynard Park, which is undergoing changes
for the good (of the many) (who are coming in droves).
Thirty CDs valued at $300, a diaper bag valued at $30,
a purse valued at $20 and sunglasses valued at $10
filched from a vehicle of undisclosed make
in the driveway of a home on Croton Lane. The
diaper bag (used) recovered later. Jewelry, pants,
bras, pajamas and accessories valued at $612
whipped from Belks at the Mall at Shelter Cove.
The items were (abandoned by lovers) (pants too
tight, jealous boy friend) (speculation: strike that)
recovered. A Dell Inspiron 9300 laptop valued
at $3,500 snatched from the realty office where
Snow Birds shed excess (in Canadian dollars).
There were no rapes or murders yesterday
(except those happening abroad). We apologize
for any inconvenience in having so little to report.

NEUROPATHY

Sometimes it starts down the leg like a trail of
gunpowder someone has just lit. A fizz in the nerves.
A child's rake scraping down the calf. Waking before dawn:
joints tingle, a motion always there, behind the knees,
the stride under the covers, a place to get to that has no name,
no sidewalks, no address. Where the mower ran over my foot
the year we went to Venice, big toe broken, the bells gonging
over the Grand Canal, something is pulling, screaming.
As if this were about travel, what my brother couldn't feel
on the Queen Mary, in the dead soles of his feet,
sailing for Rio, knowing somewhere there's dancing
in the streets. Soft sand the worst, its aftermath, 3 A.M.:
the tide's humor churning an instep, cramped arch,
as I long for the tamped-down, the firm, the made
path where moonlight hardens into long, silvery tiles.

FEAST

After the painting by Jonathan Green

The heads of three pigs arranged like cabbages
on the platter near the kettle, a man and woman
working at a wooden tub filled with blood—white
geese with necks outstretched in the shadows of
tall red barrels. Slaughter and hunger the twin
joys of the river just out of sight, rippling *love*
and *kill*, what bristles on a hide, what clotted
nostrils: two men and a boy in boots and rubber
aprons scrape clean the three skinned carcasses
hanging from a pole. Another boy who looks away,
who feels the eyes demanding something of him
that will take him out of the frame, out of the flexed
interior he inhabits like the inside of muscle, not the
small room of words, not the bedraggled tide and jagged
shells of our attention that tumble toward him, as he
carries a three-branched limb on his way toward the
kettle that is just beginning to boil. There is a child
between the women, each woman with a bowl of blood,
stripping intestines and liver, a mother's head rag the
same color as the liquid imbruing her hands, red
barrels leaning empty and yawning. A song arising
like another shade of green, different from the leaves
of camellias and live oaks—the twilight lyric taking a life.

First, the getting there—the hurtle down I-95,
an overnight in West Palm Beach, pork chops
and salads in Duffy's Sports Bar, every portal
a fume and flash of thigh, the air heavy with beery
sex, TV flickering scores, a spine crunching in a
fullback's tackle. Is it fatigue, to hear the body
counts from IED's outside Baghdad and order
more wine? The morning brings construction,
girders raw as bone, such thump and swerve as
the medic's Humvee carting off the wounded,

something already dropped horribly into a pail.
Across Boynton Blvd to Florida's Turnpike,
gated communities, miles of scorched skin. Green
coconuts drop like skulls. How many orthopedists
make a village walk? Every stop, it's pee and fill.
At last, the Keys, driving through the hologram
of *Key Largo*, Bogart's grimace rippling along the
fender like a soft fabric. In the head, in the lost dark,
in the mist, how many conch chowders in Marathon,
how many gaps in the old railroad bridge torn into

by the hurricane of '35? The green sea keeps adding,
keeps count, keeps unloading tourists from towering
cruise ships. Key West now accreted with spindle
palms, bougainvillea, oleander, the petals that are
leaves transformed, each parking space a rectangle
painted on macadam like a surgeon's mark. The drawn

names of those who thrived here long gone, long washed out
from the weedy ledge of the Casa Marina,
where further down the sands, a poet once walked
behind a woman singing beyond the genius of the sea.

FOR THE UMPTEENTH TIME

Again, again! The teal evening sky crisscrossed
by white jet streams. An elderly man's kite tilting
in the southern breeze, its tail fluttering. I thank
you and I thank you among the piles of sea foam
like fallen clouds, a shred blown away from us,
rolling and rolling, something rising to the surface,
drawn to a wet circumference. Whatever stains
the sky must be years of blood draining down
the heavens, a cry that tears open the throat in song,
joy/pain never ending. I thank you and I thank you

for that April we took the IND train to the Village,
Dylan Thomas's *Under Milkwood*, his rollicking
vowels the long surf just beginning to carry us here,
agape at the exhausted turtle scraping her eggs
into the pit beneath her. I thank you and I thank
you for the father who arrived in 1920 on Tenth
Avenue, where my grandparents and my parents
knew their only lives, your father with no language
except the feel of his hands, as I watch the horizon
collapse on Tybee Island, the light house burning

its single cell in the vast darkness of the body that is
earth and salt ocean. I thank you and I thank you
amid the turbid churning of shell and soft tissue where
night creatures open their pores and time seeps through
their being the way your kiss flooded the night
on Davidson Avenue. I thank you and I thank you

aghast at the still face in the mirror yet myself
only because you sway forever on the tide toward
me, and away again, my grief/joy threaded with
arrival and the tentacles of something quite alive.

DANCING GULL

Look at him stamping his feet as the tide
slips back: *dub-dub-dub-dub* into the soft
sand. Something dug up by his curled toes,
something he pecks and swallows, his wings
pulled to his side like a perfectly buttoned
coat. This two-step repeated each withdrawal
of wave, something near the surface now
clawed into the light and eaten, however small
its life. Years ago, what words came to mind
scooped into sentences, what un-noticeable

deaths disappeared into the white page
scrolled through a noisy platen itself
part of the chattering organism I had
become? He's at it again, *dub-dub-dub-dub*.
I hear him all night long, the soles of my feet
burning. Something forming on my tongue
small dark particles of words, something
I keep trying to say, something once not part
of me. Down near the Marriott the midnight
sea beating against a sea wall again and again.

RETURN

Packing up. Tubs of sweaters, jeans, burly coats,
our own cookware, this activity a forgetfulness,
the sea five minutes away—each folded shirt
a first flowering, a stitched intent, where the tuft-
breasted snake bird arrives every morning to stare
at the lagoon, to scan our drifting reflections
already headed for storage. Good-bye to mild
incineration on the beach. Farewell to broken TV
reception, the heron hissing past on his nightly
glide, sudden rain and thunder sweeping toward us

from Calibogue Sound to button the mouths of leaders,
untie the tourniquet around the camellia's slender
throat. Let's pile refugee shoes and books behind
the rental unit's corrugated door that slams down,
breathe the night air partly on fire in the dawn,
be cormorants drying our wings because we went
deep. Let's stop the workmen at the bridge. Let's
walk the marsh at low tide and find original mud
or repeat ourselves the way feather and scale
make a surface that slides the ether, the out-there

and the in-here, these the miles that breath travels
in the lungs. Think where creatures go to breed,
eels, penguins, salmon flailing up the falls, the small
eggs of the ruby-throated humming bird, that place
we have been years and years ago, how it calls, how
it turns away. The road, if it is a road, twisting through

honeysuckle and giant thorns, then paved and hot,
tires spinning in the trackless air like sentences
whipping round and round, making a kind of song
that rhymes at every turn and curve with home.